PUFFIN B

The BEST EVER Sleepover FUN BOOK

Books by Janet Hoggarth

THE BEST EVER SLEEPOVER FUN BOOK

HOW TO BE A DJ

The BEST EVER Sleepover FUN BOOK

Janet Hoggarth

Illustrated by Sarah Braithwaite

PUFFIN

PUFFIN BOOKS

Published by the Penguin Group
Penguin Books Ltd, 80 Strand, London WC2R 0RL, England
Penguin Group (USA) Inc., 375 Hudson Street,
New York, New York 10014, USA
Penguin Group (Canada), 90 Eglinton Avenue East, Suite 700, Toronto, Ontario,
Canada M4P 2Y3 (a division of Pearson Penguin Canada Inc.)
Penguin Ireland, 25 St Stephen's Green, Dublin 2, Ireland
(a division of Penguin Books Ltd)
Penguin Group (Australia), 250 Camberwell Road, Camberwell, Victoria 3124,
Australia (a division of Pearson Australia Group Pty Ltd)
Penguin Books India Pvt Ltd, 11 Community Centre, Panchsheel Park,
New Delhi – 110 017, India
Penguin Group (NZ), cnr Airborne and Rosedale Roads, Albany,
Auckland 1310, New Zealand (a division of Pearson New Zealand Ltd)
Penguin Books (South Africa) (Pty) Ltd, 24 Sturdee Avenue, Rosebank,
Johannesburg 2196, South Africa

Penguin Books Ltd, Registered Offices:
80 Strand, London WC2R 0RL, England

www.penguin.com

First published 2005

3

Text copyright © Puffin Books, 2005
Illustrations copyright © Sarah Braithwaite, 2005
All rights reserved

Written by Janet Hoggarth

Made and printed in England by Clays Ltd, St Ives plc

Except in the United States of America, this book is sold subject to the
condition that it shall not, by way of trade or otherwise, be lent, re-sold, hired
out, or otherwise circulated without the publisher's prior consent in any form
of binding or cover other than that in which it is published and without
a similar condition including this condition being imposed
on the subsequent purchaser

British Library Cataloguing in Publication Data
A CIP catalogue record for this book is available from the British Library

ISBN 0–141–31965–8

Contents

welcome to the Party! 1

Chapter One 2
Help! I've Never Had a Sleepover Before...
Everything you need to know about organizing your party, with brilliant ideas for themes and invitations.

Chapter Two 19
Feed Those Friends!
Cakes, canapés, cocktails, chocolate fondues... We've got the yummiest recipes – and they're fun to make too.

Chapter Three 43
Be a Makeover Queen
Transform yourselves with our beauty and make-up ideas, from fruity face masks to amazing hair creations.

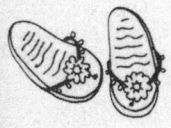

Chapter Four 59
Action Stations
Loads of ideas for gigglesome games, crafty things to make and lots, lots more...

Chapter Five 81
The Morning After
Wrap things up with the best ever breakfast and the prettiest party favours.

To my little Lilla May – I can't wait to help you with your first ever sleepover party.

welcome to the Party!

If you're reading this book then you're probably looking forward to having a sleepover soon. Or maybe you're about to go to a sleepover for the first time and don't know what to expect. What will we do? What sort of food will we eat? What games will we play? Most importantly, will we have a good time? Don't worry, this book will tell you everything that goes on at sleepovers and give you loads of ideas for things to do. We'll show you how to have the best time possible with the least amount of worry!

Now get along and start reading. You want to know how to make No-bake Chocolate Fudge Bars, don't you? And what about a blindfolded makeover? You'd love to see how that turns out, wouldn't you? How about making jewellery, stupid games to make you fall over laughing and scary stories to make you scream really loud? They're all in here waiting for you to have a go and have the best sleepover party ever!

CHAPTER ONE

Help! I've Never Had a Sleepover Before...

So Katie asked Jo, who asked Naomi, who asked you if your parents would let you have a sleepover. Eeeek! They've all had them and now it's your turn. You had a good time at theirs, but you have no idea how to organize your own, make it fun and make sure all your guests turn up. Or maybe you've never been to a sleepover before and you're *completely* clueless! Bingo! It's a good job you've got this book, then.

First things first: how do you decide what sort of things *you* want to do at the sleepover? And will they be the same things that your friends want to do? Do this simple quiz to work out a few ideas.

What's Your Sleepover Personality?

1. On a Saturday you and your friends normally:
a. Hang out and watch TV.
b. Go stunt biking or skateboarding.
c. Pool together all your clothes and stage fashion shows.
d. Draw and paint and make stuff.

2. Your favourite type of birthday party is:
a. Going to the movies, then for a pizza.
b. One with loads of action, e.g. a pool party.
c. A fancy-dress party.
d. A trip to the 'Paint Your Own Pottery' place.

3. Would you describe you and your friends as:
a. Chilled-out chicks?
b. Thrill seekers?

c. Girlie girls?
d. Arty-crafty types?

4. You are invited to a party where everyone has to bring a game or activity. You bring:
a. Your fave DVD.
b. Twister with a blindfold.
c. Lots of make-up for makeovers.
d. Beads and elastic for funky necklaces.

5. If you were a food, what would you be?
a. Pizza.
b. Spicy Thai Curry.
c. Strawberry Cheesecake.
d. Chocolate Fondue.

Let's see what your answers say about you:

Mostly As
You and your mates are laid-back kinda girls. Nothing too hectic for you! Your ideal sleepover would probably involve lots of food, a couple of cool movies and a mountain of popcorn. But don't miss out on

other ideas – we know you would love a scary story or two as well!

Mostly Bs

Hey, action girls! You love anything a bit daring, don't you? We can see you now at a sleepover, playing Truth or Dare and persuading people Twister is a good idea if you only use elbows and knees and blindfolds. Sit down for five minutes, though, and bask in the glory of having your hair teased into a glam style. You never know, you might like it!

Mostly Cs

Make-up, hair products – you can't get enough! Your bedroom looks like a Boots beauty counter. Your perfect sleepover would involve transforming everyone into total babes. You'll have to smudge that perfect lipstick if you're gonna eat your pizza, though!

Mostly Ds

You girls could make a cool handbag out of an egg box and a bit of string! You're never happier than when you are making something original or revamping old clothes. Your ideal sleepover would probably involve lots of beads, thread, glue and ribbon. Don't forget you can make food as well – get stuck into that chocolate goo!

BUT ...

In reality, you probably like doing a combination of all the things above. And that goes for the sleepover too. You can have makeovers, jewellery-making, scary stories, movies and so on, all in the same sleepover. You just might not be able to fit them all in!

Basic Guidelines for a Fab Sleepover

★ The number-one rule is that there are no rules! You can do anything you like. If you and your mates want to sit around dressed as extras from a scary movie watching repeats of *Scooby-Doo*, then so be it. Whatever rocks your world!

★ Sleepovers are best kept to small numbers or it can get out of control. So having your whole class over isn't really going to work. For a start – where will you all sleep? It's best to invite just your closest buddies.

★ Make sure your parents or guardians are completely happy about the sleepover and know all your plans. Ask nicely for their help. You will need them on standby to help you set up and make some of the food, as some of the recipes require hot ovens and boiling water. Look out for the 'Grab a grown-up' symbol on the recipe.

GRAB A GROWN-UP!

★ Set a time for the party to start and have a think about which activities you are going to do. If it helps, you can write them down. They don't have to be in the right order, but it would help to have a rough idea. For example, if you were going to watch a movie, you'd want to make sure all the popcorn and food was made before so you can pig out while goggling the box.

★ If you and your friends are totally into dressing up, why not have a themed party? Ideas for that are later in this chapter.

★ Send out a funky invite that will have people talking and desperate to come to the sleepover. Check out ideas later in this chapter too.

★ Decide on the venue for the sleepover. Will it be too crowded in your bedroom for your mates? Also, you want to be able to make some noise and not creep about all night (unless you are trying to frighten someone!). Downstairs, away from the grown-ups, is usually best.

★ Do you want to decorate the sleepover room? You don't have to, but it might create a good atmosphere, especially if you're going to tell ghost stories! Look out for ideas in this chapter.

★ Make sure you get everyone to bring their own bedding, sleeping bags and so on. The hostess usually bags the sofa but, as we said before, there are no rules! You can use camp beds or inflatable mattresses if you don't fancy the floor. It's not a bad idea to put down as many mattresses, cushions or beanbags as you can before everyone settles down for the night – bare floors can start to feel pretty uncomfortable in the small hours. Make sure you've got enough space for everyone to sleep!

★ Don't feel you have to do loads of activities to make it a fun night. Having too much to do will be stressy – you want to be able to chill and enjoy it. Go with the flow. If something you planned doesn't happen, it's only because everyone was having too much of a good time to fit it in!

★ Make sure you get lots of sleep the night before!

★ Always, always have breakfast ingredients bought and ready for the morning. You will be starving from all the activity, even if it's only a few hours since you last ate.

Ideas for Themed Parties and Decorations

★ Spooky sleepovers are always fun, especially if your party happens around Halloween time. Get everyone to dress up as witches, ghosts or whatever they want. You could decorate the living room with bats and spiders from the joke shop. Get a grown-up to make a jack-o'-lantern from a pumpkin and light it with a torch (candles would be too dangerous). Make fake tombstones from large pieces of grey card and prop them up

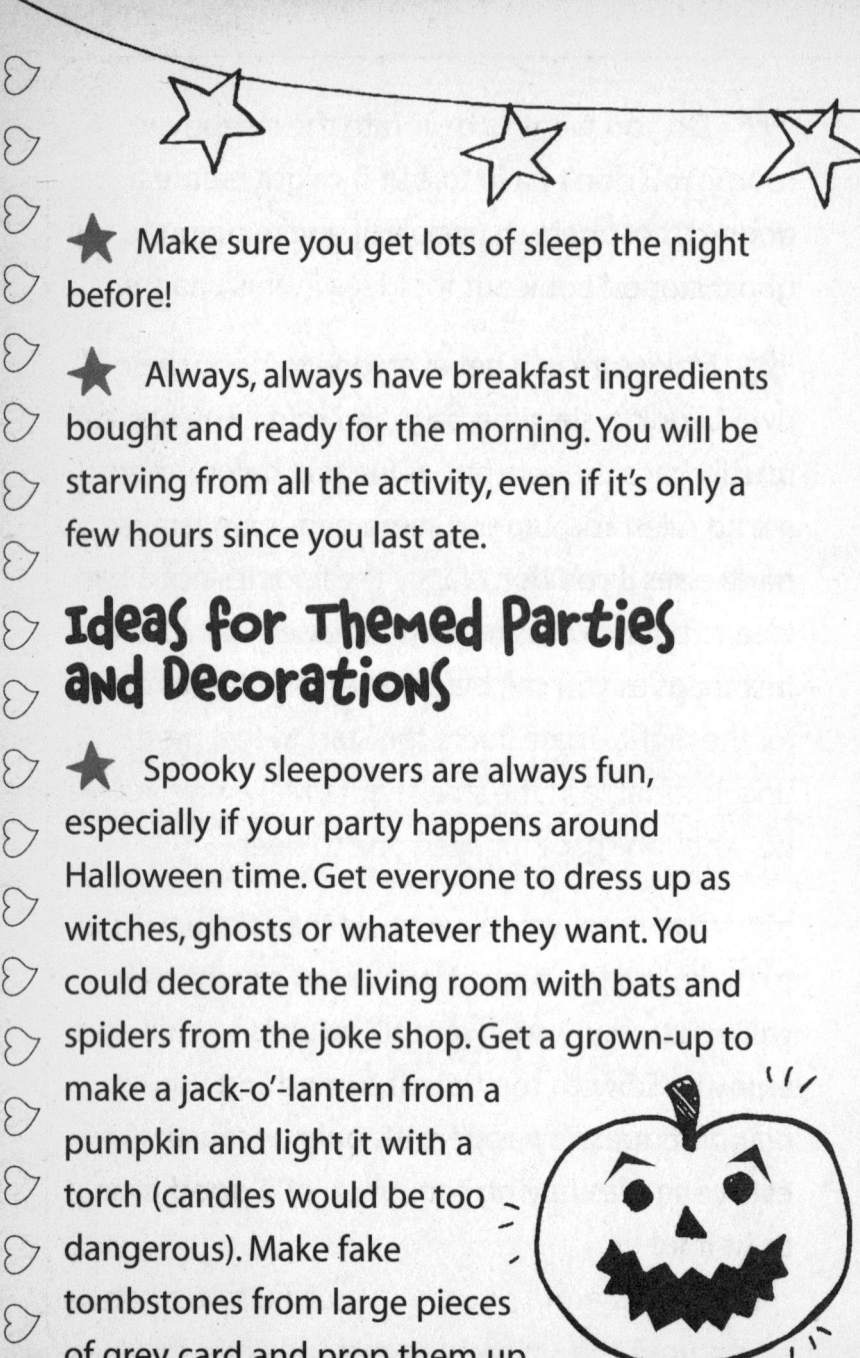

around the room, so it feels like you are in a graveyard. Spooky!

★ Why not try a pop-star party – where everyone comes dressed as their favourite pop star. Decorate the room with fairy lights. You might even be able to persuade your parents to hire some disco lights for the night! Put up posters of all your fave stars around the room to inspire you later for the karaoke competition.

★ How about a Hawaiian luau? 'Luau' is the Hawaiian word for 'party' – ideal for a summer sleepover. You can dress up in swimsuits or bikinis, wear grass skirts (you can buy them in party shops) or sarongs and wear leis (flower garlands) round your necks. They are very easy to make. Cut out lots of flowers from different-coloured paper or card and make a hole in the centre with a hole punch or scissors. Thread one flower on to a piece of string, followed by a piece of macaroni and then another flower, and so on, until the string is almost full, then tie the ends. *Voilà* – a lei for each of your guests. Get ready for that limbo dance later!

★ Everyone loves *Finding Nemo* and *The Little Mermaid*, so why not have an Under the Sea party? Dress up as mermaids, fish, octopus or sharks – anything to do with the sea. Decorate the room with cut-out fishes, shells and seaweed made from green card. Hang blue and green balloons everywhere with lots of silver gift ribbon curling off them like water sprays. Make fish mobiles from silver card and hang them from the ceiling. The place will look like a fish tank!

★ Bad-taste parties are a real giggle. Everyone comes in the

most hideous clothes with clashing colours and odd shoes. You could have bad-taste makeovers and eat foul-looking food that really tastes nice. Get handy with that food colouring!

Impressive Invites

This will be the first impression your friends get of the fun to come. So you'd better make it a good one! Always include the date and start time of the party, the theme (if there is one), what to bring, e.g. bedding, a board game, make-up and so on, and the pick-up time in the morning.

Princess Tiara

You will need: a piece of plain card, gold card, glitter, sequins and stick-on jewels, a silver pen, scissors, glue.

✳ Make a template of a tiara or a crown by drawing the shape on a piece of plain card and carefully cutting it out.

✳ Place your template on the gold card and then draw round it as many times as you need to for your guests. Cut out your invites.

✳ Now for the best part – decorating them. Write the party details on the back of each invite in silver pen, then turn it over and go mad with the glitter, jewels and sequins. Make each one a little bit different for each friend.

So Sweet

You will need: lots of different funky-coloured sweets, e.g. Jelly Babies, Fruit Pastilles, Midget Gems or Dolly Mixtures, coloured card, strong glue, felt tips, scissors.

♡ It's best to use a simple shape, such as a rectangle, for this invite. So cut out as many rectangles as you need from the coloured card.

♡ Glue the sweets in any order you fancy round the edge of the invite to make a pretty border.

♡ When the sweets are stuck hard, write the party details in the centre of the sweet frame with different-coloured felt tips.

♡ If you want to make the invite look really cool, you could seal the sweets with some clear varnish.

Chocolate Bar

This is so easy and effective! You will need: as many bars of choc as there are guests, A4 gold-coloured paper, glue.

☆ Make a label template on a computer, if you have access to one. If you're not sure what to do, ask a grown-up. Type in the details of the party and print them out on the gold-coloured paper. Or you could use ordinary sticky labels.

GRAB A GROWN-UP!

☆ Cut out the labels and stick them to the front of the chocolate bars. If you can't use a computer, just write out the details on the gold paper instead and cut to size, ready to stick on.

FLUFFY HEART

You will need: a piece of plain card, some pink or red card, a gold pen, pink feathers or an old feather boa, scissors, glue.

✳ Make a heart template by drawing the shape on the piece of plain card and carefully cutting it out.

✳ Place your template on the coloured card and then draw round it as many times as you need to for your guests. Cut out your heart shapes.

✳ Stick the feathers round the edge of each heart.

✳ When the glue is dry, write the party info in the centre with your gold pen. Easy!

You will find templates for the heart, pillowcase and lip invites on pages 89–90. You can cut them straight from the book or photocopy them.

Pillowcase

You will need: a piece of plain card, lots of different-coloured card, scissors, glue, felt tips.

♡ Draw and cut out a pillow template from the plain card – a rectangle with pillow-shaped soft edges.

♡ Use your template and the coloured card to make your invites. This time, cut out twice as many pillow shapes as there are guests. Make mini 'pillowcases' by gluing down two long edges and one short edge of each shape. Stick two shapes together, making sure that one end is left unglued and open, just like a real pillowcase.

♡ You now need to make the pillow to put inside. Just cut out a smaller rectangle that can slip in the pillowcase envelope really easily. Write the party details on that.

♡ It's time to decorate the pillowcase. You can do anything you want: stripes, dots, flowers, bears and so on. You can even use glitter.

Luscious Lips

(Good for a makeover sleepover!)

You will need: a piece of plain card, red or pink card, scissors, high gloss or clear nail varnish, a paintbrush, a black pen.

♡ Make a mouth template from the plain card.

♡ Using the red card, draw round the template as many times as there are guests.

♡ Draw a lip line down the middle of each mouth to make the lips seem real.

♡ Turn over and, on the back, write out the party info.

♡ Next, varnish the 'lips' to make them nice and glossy, being careful not to get any on yourself. It will take a while to dry, but it will be worth it!

Other Quick Ideas:

♡ A microphone for a pop-star party.

♡ Giant flowers for a Hawaiian luau.

♡ Witch's hat, bats, spiders and orange pumpkin shapes for Halloween.

♡ Fish or shells for Under the Sea.

Chapter Two

Feed Those Friends!

No self-respecting sleepover would be complete without a mass of food to scoff. So here's the deal – have lots and keep the guests happy! Check out some of these tasty treats to get your taste buds going. Some of the recipes are fun to make on the night, but others might be better made beforehand.* Don't feel you have to make all the food, though! Just having one or two home-made things will give your party that special touch.

✶ Don't forget to look out for the 'Grab a grown-up' symbol for that much-needed adult helping hand.

GRAB A GROWN-UP!

SAVOURY MUNCHIES

Mini Pizza Tarts

It's best to make these before everyone arrives.

You will need:

GRAB A GROWN-UP!

1 pack of ready-made puff pastry
for every four guests

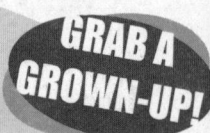

You will need the following ingredients for each pack of pastry you use. Increase the amounts for each additional pack.

3 tablespoons tomato purée and 2
of sun-dried tomato purée
1 tablespoon of garlic purée
1 teaspoon of dried oregano
500 g of baby tomatoes, chopped in half
2 red onions, cut into rings
400 g cubed feta cheese or cubed
mozzarella cheese

Plus:
1 runny egg yolk
Olive oil and balsamic vinegar
Flour for rolling

- Preheat the oven to 230°C/450°F/Gas Mark 8.
- Roll out each puff-pastry slab into a rectangular shape, just under 1 cm thick.
- Cut each large rectangle into four equal-sized rectangles. Place them on greased baking trays (try not to cram them together too much).
- To make the sauce, mix the three purées together in a bowl. Add about a tablespoon of olive oil, the oregano and some splashes of balsamic vinegar, and give it a good stir. Shake a little salt and pepper on too.
- Next, lightly score a 2-cm frame round the inside edges of each rectangle with a knife. This will be the tart crust. Now paint on the egg yolk with a pastry brush or your very clean fingers!
- Spread the tomato mixture inside the tart crust without touching the egg yolk.
- Time to get busy with the tomatoes, placing them on top of the mixture, cut side up. Next, fling on the onion rings and distribute the cheese evenly between all the tarts, leaving the crust clean.

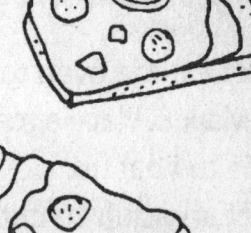

- Drizzle on some olive oil and they are ready for the oven!
- Place in the oven until the tarts have risen and are a golden-brown colour. You can eat them hot or cold. Mmmmm!

Potato-Skin Dippers

Put these in the oven when you want to eat them, as they are better hot. Or you could make them earlier and zap them in the microwave for a few minutes to heat them up.

You will need:
Large baking potatoes (approx. 1 per person)
Olive oil
Salt and pepper
A sprinkle of cayenne pepper if you like them spicy!

GRAB A GROWN-UP!

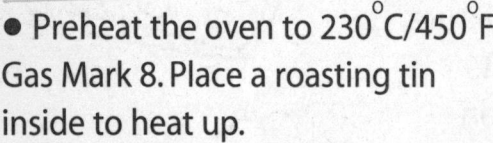

- Preheat the oven to 230°C/450°F/Gas Mark 8. Place a roasting tin inside to heat up.

- Get an adult to cut the potatoes in half lengthways and then into four lengths if the potatoes are big enough, so they resemble large chips.

- Rinse the potato pieces well and pat dry on kitchen paper. Next, place them in a large mixing bowl and drizzle olive oil over them until generously coated. Season with salt and pepper and the cayenne if you want it.
- Toss the potatoes in the oil – it is easier to do this with your hands. Greasy!
- Take the roasting tin out with oven gloves. Tip the potatoes in and place back in the oven. They should sizzle nicely. Cook until golden brown and tender in the middle – about 20 minutes.
- Now all you need are some dips!

Tomato and Cheese Dip

You will need:
200 g cream cheese
2-3 tablespoons mayonnaise
1 tablespoon of tomato ketchup
A few dashes of Worcester sauce
A few dashes of soy sauce
6 cherry tomatoes, chopped into eighths
A small handful of chopped chives
Freshly ground pepper

Dipping Tip!

If you are having a Halloween party you can add green food colouring to cheese and chive dip to make it look like snot – nice! Other dips you can try from the supermarket are hummus, guacamole, tzatziki and taramasalata. You can also chop up cucumber, carrot, peppers or pitta bread and dip in crackers.

- Just mix all the ingredients together in a bowl and chill in the fridge.
- For cheese and chive dip just leave out the tomatoes, tomato sauce, soy sauce and Worcester sauce.

Chunky Tomato Salsa

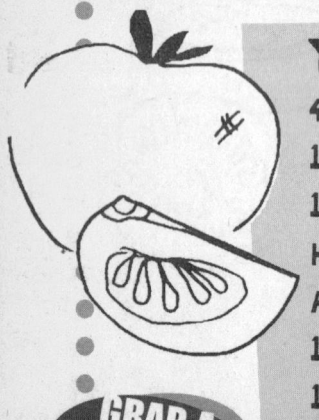

GRAB A GROWN-UP!

You will need:
400 g tin chopped tomatoes
1 tablespoon of tomato purée
1 small red onion
Half a red pepper
A squeeze of lime juice
1 heaped teaspoon of brown sugar
1 tablespoon of chopped coriander
A sprinkling of cayenne pepper
A sprinkling of salt
Kitchen towel

- First of all, chop the onion and pepper into really small pieces, then place in a bowl with a little salt and cover them in boiling water. Leave for about five minutes to soften.
- Drain the onion and pepper mixture carefully in a colander and empty on to a piece of kitchen towel. Dry the pieces off. Put them into a big bowl and mix with all the other ingredients, seasoning with salt and pepper. Leave in the fridge till you want to dip.

Sticky Chicken Drummers

GRAB A GROWN-UP!

Marinate these on the morning of the party to make sure they taste extra yummy.

You will need:

As many chicken drumsticks as necessary
1 small onion, finely chopped
2 cloves garlic, minced
4 tablespoons of tomato purée
1 tablespoon of olive oil
1 tablespoon of brown sugar
Half a tablespoon of balsamic vinegar
1 teaspoon of dried oregano

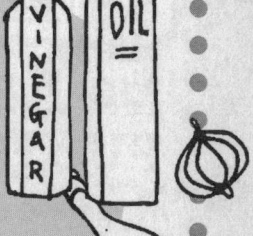

- Fry the onion in the oil until soft and add the sugar, cooking for a few minutes.
- Next, add the rest of the ingredients and let them simmer for about 5 minutes.

- Put the goo into a bowl and toss in the drumsticks (this recipe will coat about eight to ten). Leave in the fridge to marinate until you need them.

- Preheat the grill and place the drummers in a baking dish – you will probably have to do them in two batches. Turn the chicken after about 8–10 minutes and add more sauce. Grill for a further 8–10 minutes on the other side until cooked thoroughly. You can eat them hot or cold.
- If you are allowed, these taste even better on the barbecue!

sweet-toothed treats

No-bake chocolate fudge bars

GRAB A GROWN-UP

These are enormously popular at sleepovers and are fun to make on the night, with all of you helping out in the kitchen. But you'll have to wait a while for them to cool down before you can eat them!

You will need:

100 g dark chocolate
100 g butter
425 g can of condensed milk
450 g caster sugar
8–10 shortbread biscuits, broken into chunks
Icing sugar for dusting

- Grease a 20 cm square baking tin.
- Put the butter, sugar and condensed milk into a large pan. Heat gently until the sugar has dissolved, then bring to the boil for five minutes.
- You must keep stirring all the time. Once the mixture starts coming away from the sides of the pan and has turned a darker colour, add the chocolate in chunks.
- When the choc has melted, you can start adding pieces of biscuit. If you don't want to add all the biscuit, you don't have to. This is just a guide. You might want more fudge than biscuit!
- Pour the hot mixture into the tin and leave to cool at room temperature. Try not to taste it as you will burn your mouth!
- Just before the fudge turns cold,

mark it into bars with a knife and when it is completely cold, get a grown-up to cut it properly.

• While the bars are still in the tin, sift a layer of icing sugar over them for that finishing touch. YUM!

Naughty Fairy Cakes

These are fun for any sleepover, but especially good for a Halloween or bad-taste party!

You will need:

175 g self-raising flour
175 g softened butter or margarine
175 g sugar
3 eggs, beaten
Green food colouring
18 paper cake cases

GRAB A GROWN-UP!

For the icing:
Orange food colouring
100 g icing sugar
1–2 tablespoons of lemon juice
Smarties

• Preheat the oven to 190°C/375°F/Gas Mark 5.

- Beat the butter and sugar together in a bowl with a wooden spoon until blended, then add the flour and beat well.
- Next, beat in the eggs until the mixture is nice and smooth. Or you could just whizz everything in a food processor until you get the same result.
- Now for the fun part: you have to add a few drops of green food colouring, just enough to make the mixture resemble something bubbling in a witch's pot!

- Put the cake cases into bun trays and drop the mixture in the cases with a teaspoon.
- Bake for 12–15 minutes or until the cakes have risen and feel springy when you touch them.

- Only ice the cakes when they have completely cooled. To make the lemon icing, sift the icing sugar into a large bowl. Then add the lemon juice gradually, mixing it the whole time until you have a paste runny enough to coat each little cake.

- Add a few drops of orange food colouring to get that nice bright orange colour that goes so well with green!

- Place Smarties on the top of each cake. (Not the orange ones, though – the colours are supposed to clash. You'll have to eat those first!) They are ready for scoffing!

Grilled Fruit Kebabs

These are also great done on the barbecue if you are allowed, but under the grill is cool too. Excellent for a Hawaiian luau sleepover.

You will need:
Different kinds of fruit – softish fruits are best, e.g. pineapple, strawberries, kiwi fruit, banana, satsuma, grapes, raspberries, peaches...
Icing sugar for dusting
Wooden or metal skewers
Ice cream and maple syrup to serve

- If you use wooden skewers, soak them in water for a bit to stop them burning under the grill.
- Wash the fruit and chop up the larger fruit into smaller chunks. Start threading all the fruits

on to the skewers. These look (and taste) great with different colour combos – a green grape followed by a red strawberry, then a banana slice and so on.

• When all the skewers are full, dust them with icing sugar and place under a preheated hot grill. Keep turning them until the fruit has cooked slightly and is starting to look a bit toasty!

• Serve with ice cream and maple syrup – YUM!

Sleepover Chocolate-goo Fondue

A great dish to share on a sleepover, this has to be made on the night. Get everyone to bring their favourite type of chocolate bar to add to the pot. (Ones without biscuits or nuts in them are best.)

You will need:
GRAB A GROWN-UP!

Lots of chocolate bars
Fruit, marshmallows, plain biscuits for dipping
Toothpicks or skewers to aid dipping
Wipes to clean off those sticky fingers!

- Chop or break the bars into manageable chunks.
- Grab a pan, set it on a low heat and gradually add the chocolate bits.
- See what happens! The final mixture is made up of so many different chocolate bars that you won't know exactly how it will taste until you've added them all. We're pretty sure it'll be scrumptious, though!
- When the goo has melted and you've stirred it about with a wooden spoon, pour it into a warmed large bowl and start dipping before it sets rock hard. You can also use it as a yummy sauce to go with ice cream.

canapés

Canapés are mini pieces of finger food that celebrities eat at their cool parties. They are nearly always served on silver trays by waiters. Here are a few ideas to make your sleepover the poshest party in town.

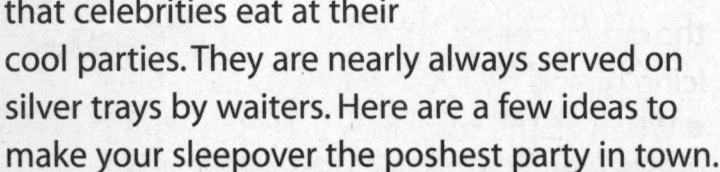

To get your silver trays at a fraction of the price,

just head to the nearest supermarket and buy those large silver foil platters from the section that has all the paper plates and cups. If you want to be even swankier, buy some paper doilies as well! Arrange all your canapés beautifully on the platters and offer them to your guests. If you can persuade a younger sibling to be the waiter (bribed with food), brilliant; if not, ask a parent or do it yourself!

Cream Cheese Baby Toms

You will need:
Lots of cherry tomatoes
1 large tub of cream cheese
A handful of snipped chives

GRAB A GROWN-UP!

- Chop all the tomatoes in half and scoop out the seeds.
- Next, fill each tomato half with cream cheese. Now, if you want to be really posh you can pipe the cream cheese into the tomatoes using an icing piping bag. Ask a grown-up to help!
- When all the tomatoes are filled, sprinkle over the chopped chives and arrange nicely on a silver platter.

Mini cheese on toast

GRAB A GROWN-UP!

You will need:
Sliced white and brown bread
Any block of hard cheese, e.g. cheddar
Pastry cutters

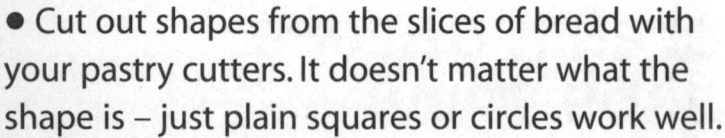

- Cut out shapes from the slices of bread with your pastry cutters. It doesn't matter what the shape is – just plain squares or circles work well.
- Next, slice the cheese and cut out shapes with the cutters. If you have a smaller version of the shape you chose for the bread, use that. If not, use the same cutter as before.
- Toast one side of the shaped bread under the grill. Once that is toasted, turn it over and place the matching cheese shape on top.
- Grill until the cheese is bubbling and before the bread burns!
- Serve straight away on a posh platter.

Mini pinwheel sweets and savouries

You will need:
1 pack of ready-made puff pastry
1 jar of yeast extract
75 g grated cheese

For the sweet version:
1 pack of ready-made puff pastry
1 pack of ready-made marzipan
Raspberry jam
Flour for rolling

GRAB A GROWN-UP!

- Preheat the oven to 220°C/350°F/Gas Mark 8.
- Roll out the pastry on a floured surface into a large rectangle, about 1 cm thick.
- For the savoury pinwheels, spread a thin layer of yeast extract over the whole rectangle, then scatter the grated cheese on top.
- Roll the pastry into a long sausage (a bit like a Swiss roll) and chill for half an hour until firm.
- For the sweet pinwheels, roll out the marzipan block till it is roughly the same size as the pastry. It will be a lot thinner.

- Spread a layer of jam over the pastry and place the marzipan on top, cutting off any overhanging edges.
- As above, roll into a sausage and chill.
- Next, cut your sausage into lots of 1-cm slices, place them on a greased baking tray and cook until the pastry is slightly browned. If you're making both recipes, keep the savouries and sweets separate on the baking trays, as the cheese and jam will ooze out and make a right gooey mess!

Tiny Kebabs for Dipping

These go brilliantly with the dips at the beginning of the chapter. Just put the dip in a small bowl – and place in the middle of a silver platter. Arrange the kebabs round the dip.

You will need:
Baby tomatoes, cut into quarters
Small cubes of cheese
Carrots and cucumber cut into cubes
Peppers cut into squares
Olives (if you like them)
Cocktail sticks

- All you need to do is stick the veggies and cheese on to the sticks.
- Make lots of variations as there is no way you will fit more than three pieces on to each stick!

Impressive yet Easy Ideas

- Slice up shop-bought quiches and tarts into small bite-sized squares and serve on the silver platters. Pizzas are also a good idea, cut into mini pieces.
- Buy mini muffins from the supermarket and arrange on the platters with cut-up strawberries and dusted icing sugar.
- Dip lots of strawberries in melted chocolate and leave to harden in the fridge. Arrange on the platters with mint leaves and a dusting of icing sugar.
- Make cucumber sandwiches and cut them out with pastry cutters in lots of fancy shapes.
- Mini Chinese spring rolls also make good canapés as well as onion bhajis and samosas.
- Don't forget to have a supply of paper napkins at the ready!

IT'S COCKTAIL HOUR!

No party is a party without exotic drinks. You can drink cola and lemonade any time – but you need something special for your sleepover! Why not buy some plastic wine glasses from the supermarket to serve your drinks in – just right for you sophisticated party animals! To add extra glamour, dip the rim of the glass first in a saucer of lemon juice, then in a saucer of caster sugar, for instant cocktail frosting! You can buy pretty cocktail umbrellas at party shops or some supermarkets. Straws and stirrers are also a must.

> For fancy ice cubes you can freeze Jelly Babies, Smarties, clean rose petals, raspberries and so on in the water in the ice-cube trays!

Banana Boat

You will need:
2 ripe bananas
1 can of coconut milk
Pineapple juice

GRAB A GROWN-UP!

- Chop the bananas and blend them in a blender or with a wand blender in a bowl. Or you could press them through a sieve into a bowl.
- Add the coconut milk and mix/blend well, then add pineapple juice to taste. You may want lots or just a little. Blend well again and serve chilled with a slice of lime on the side of the glass.

Strawberry Fizz

You will need:
Lots of strawberries
Sugar
Soda water

GRAB A GROWN-UP!

- Chop the strawberries into quarters and place them in a pan. Sprinkle with at least 2 tablespoons of sugar. You may want more if you have a ton of strawberries.
- Next, cover them with just enough water and let them simmer until the fruit is soft.

- When the strawberries are cooked through, mash them up or put them in a blender. Then pour the pulp into a bowl to chill in the fridge.
- When cold, place a few scoops of the pulp in a glass and top up with soda water. Add ice and a sprig of mint to decorate.

Cola Float

This traditional American sleepover drink will fill you up.

You will need:
Vanilla ice cream
Cola

- Place 2 scoops of vanilla ice cream into a tall glass and fill it up with cola. It's up to you whether you drink through a straw or eat it with a spoon! Why not do both?

Strawberry and Banana Crush

You will need:
Lots of ice cubes
Vanilla ice cream
Strawberries and ripe bananas

GRAB A GROWN-UP!

- Whizz the ice in a blender till it is crushed, then add some mashed banana and chopped strawberries.
- Whizz until they are mushed up with the ice.
- Finally, add a few scoops of ice cream and give it a final whizz. It doesn't matter about quantities – you can just experiment!
- Pour into glasses and drink through a straw.

Peach Punch

You will need:
1 carton of peach juice
1 carton of orange juice
Half a carton of cranberry juice
Juice of 1 lime
1 peach, cut into slices

- Mix all the ingredients together in a big bowl and serve in frosted glasses with posh ice cubes.

Yoghurt Smoothies

For these, you can throw any soft fruit into the blender and top up with yoghurt – a healthy alternative to the ice-cream version. Add milk to make the smoothie runnier.

GRAB A GROWN-UP!

Chocolate-bar Shake

This is the same principle as the chocolate-bar fondue.

You will need:
milk
chocolate bars

GRAB A GROWN-UP!

- Melt the chosen bars in a pan, very slowly.
- When the chocolate has just melted, gradually add the milk, whisking it to blend all the milk and chocolate together.
- You could drink this hot, but it is even better served chilled with a scoop of chocolate ice cream.

Cocktail Free-for-all

Just ask the grown-ups if you can have lots of different fruit juices and fizzy drinks and experiment with different combos in the kitchen. You may well invent a new drink that is so delicious everyone goes mad for it. Or you could end up tipping it down the sink! That's the exciting part – you just never know …

CHAPTER THREE
Be a Makeover Queen

No sleepover would be complete without trying your hand at transforming yourselves into sleeping beauties. Use these face-pack and make-up ideas to glam up your sleepover.

Store-cupboard Face Packs

These are the best. You can make them up together in the kitchen and then laugh at each other's gooey faces! The packs can be a bit messy, so it is probably easier to apply them in the bathroom or kitchen or put down some towels if you are in the living room.

Banana and Avocado
(For dry to normal skin)

YOU WILL NEED:
1 ripe banana
1 ripe avocado
3 tablespoons fine oatmeal
2 tablespoons live natural yoghurt
1 tablespoon honey

* First, cleanse your face with soap or cleanser and make sure you have tied your hair out of the way.
* Mash the banana and avocado together and mix in the honey, yoghurt and oatmeal.
* Apply the mush quite thickly to your face and neck, avoiding the eye area. There should be enough for about three or four of you.
* Lie back and relax for 10 minutes with cold slices of cucumber on your eyes.
* Next, wipe off the mush with warm water and a face flannel. You will have a healthy glow and your skin will tingle!

Nourishing Mask
(For any skin type)
YOU WILL NEED:
2 egg yolks
2 tablespoons honey
3 drops almond oil

* Mix the egg yolks well and beat in the other ingredients.
* Pat the mixture on your cleansed face and leave for 20 minutes.
* Rinse off with cool water.

Strawberry Delight
(For oily skin)

YOU WILL NEED:
6 strawberries
1 egg white
Trickle of honey

✻ Beat the egg white until it is slightly frothy.
✻ Mush the strawberries to a pulp and then add the egg white and honey. Mix well.
✻ Apply to clean face and leave for 20 minutes to work its magic.
✻ Rinse off with warm water.

Now you have your beautiful glowing skin, it's time to undo all the good work and slap on some war paint!

See if you can borrow a large mirror from your parents or guardian and wind fairy lights round the edge to make it fit for a Hollywood star. Lean it against a wall or on a chair and use it as Makeover Central.

> **Top Tip!**
> Save tea bags for the week running up to the sleepover and store them in the fridge. These make great eye masks.

MAKE-UP MUST-HAVES

When you send out the invites for the sleepover, don't forget to ask your mates to bring along their make-up so that you have plenty of different items and colours to choose from. As well as eyeshadows, blusher and lipsticks, see if you can get hold of:

* Make-up wipes – you will be wiping off and reapplying different looks all night. They save on mess and are quick and easy.
* Lipgloss – clear and coloured. You can never have too much!
* Glitter, bronzer, body jewellery and bindis. Jewels look cool dotted along one cheek or on your chest like a necklace.
* Eyeliners and lipliners
* Mascara (if you are feeling brave!)
* Vaseline
* Cotton ear buds

If you don't know where to start and wonder what colours might suit you, try these basic colour ideas for skin tones . . .

Eye Secrets

What suits your eye colour?
Blue eyes: try shades of blue (but not the same as your eye colour), different browns, shimmery white, lilac or pink.
Green or hazel eyes: peach, mauve, shimmery gold, purple/pinks and silver all look great on you.
Brown eyes: shimmery golds and bronzes look great on you, as do stronger colours, such as greens and plums.

✷ Try using just one colour at first on the actual eyelid and then a lighter colour underneath your eyebrow. Use different combinations and get really adventurous.

✷ If you have a steady hand, draw a line on your top lid right next to your lashes with your chosen eyeliner. Starting from the outer edge of the lid work your way inwards until you have outlined the whole lid. If the line is very shaky (which it probably will be), just smudge it gently with a cotton ear bud for that smoky-eyed look!

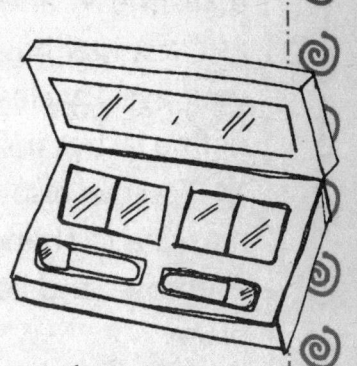

* Mascara is optional as it can be really messy and leave you looking as if a spider has set up home on your eye. Try clear mascara to define lashes instead.

* You can also use the clear mascara to shape your eyebrows and keep them in place.

* But, of course, feel free to ignore all this and opt for a rainbow of colours if you want! Also, trying lots of different looks will help you see what really suits you, as no one can really tell until it is on their face for real.

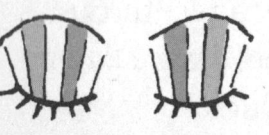

Top Tip!

If you are going to go crazy with the paint palette on your eyes, go easy on the lips and cheeks. Keep it simple elsewhere with just a clear gloss and a dusting of blusher. You don't want to end up looking like an accident in a make-up factory, do you?

Lips and cheeks

Fair skin: pinky-brown lipsticks and gloss and a warm pink blusher. But bright red lipstick can look fabbo too.

Asian skin: dark reddish brown lips or deep purple-pink and beige blusher.

Medium and olive skin: deep pink or plum lips and peach-brown blusher.

Black skin: deep plum, bright red or brown lips and plum blusher.

✲ Apply blusher on the apples of your cheeks. To find the best place, pinch your cheeks and smile at the same time. Dab on blusher where you are pink.

✲ Bronzer makes you look like you have a healthy glow from sitting in the sun, but without the skin-damaging rays. Take a blusher brush and brush bronzer on the bridge of your nose, forehead and cheekbones for a sun-kissed complexion.

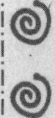

Top Tip!

If you have chapped lips or just want to make sure your smackers are perfectly smooth before you apply anything, try this simple trick. Smear your lips with Vaseline and brush them gently with an old toothbrush to get rid of any flaky skin. Wipe it off to reveal velvety lips.

✱ For perfect lips, outline them first in a lipliner which is a similar colour to the lipstick or slightly lighter.

✱ Next, paint on a layer of colour using a lip brush (if you have one). Or apply lipstick carefully (and not too heavily) straight from the holder.

✱ Blot your lips on a tissue and repeat. Dot lipgloss on just the centre of both bottom and top lips and press together. Much more than that and you will look like an oil slick!

✱ Try mixing different colours together, using a brush to get new combinations, with your palm as the palette.

Novelty Nails

For luscious nails, just follow these simple pointers:

✻ Before you start painting on colours, you need to do a bit of tidying! Soak your fingers in warm soapy water for a few minutes, then pat dry.

✻ Take an orange stick (looks like a lollipop stick!) and gently push back the cuticles on each nail.

✻ Massage in hand cream when you have finished and then file away rough edges with an emery board. File in one direction only, as a sawing action can split the nails.

✻ Choose your colour, then sweep the varnish once up the centre of the nail first. Start just above the cuticle, painting up to the tip, then do the same again, once on either side.

✻ Apply a second coat as soon as the first is dry.

✻ For two-tone or three-tone nails, paint on one stripe of colour, let it dry, then paint each side with different colours. Apply a top coat of clear varnish to seal it properly.

* Nail jewels, bindis, transfers and tattoos are all fun to try out as well.
* When painting your toenails, stick twists of tissue paper between each nail to stop the varnish sticking to your toes.
* Any splodges on fingers and toes can easily be wiped away with an ear bud dipped in nail-varnish remover.

Top Tip!

For a cheap and easy hand/foot scrub just take a few tablespoons of almond oil and sprinkle in some sea salt. Now massage into your hands and nails like you are washing them with soap. Rinse off. For feet, add a few drops of tea-tree oil to invigorate your tootsies and stop them ponging!

Temporary Tattoos

Body art is another cool sleepover activity. Instead of buying those fake tattoos (though you can use those as well) why not draw your own, using the make-up you already have from the makeovers?

✽ Clean the skin with a wipe first and let it dry. Draw the outline in a darker colour using lipliners or eyeliners, and fill in with eyeshadows, glitter, lipstick, blusher, jewels and so on.

✽ Copy cartoon characters from comics and magazines or make up your own designs. Draw everything on paper first to get it right.

✽ Simple ideas are hearts, flowers, fish, eyes, stars or moons – easy shapes. You can try out things like butterflies, dolphins, cats and so on when you have got the hang of it.

✽ To seal the design, lightly spritz with hairspray (not if it is on your face, though!).

Hair-raising styles

There will always be a budding hairdresser at any sleepover, guaranteed! Get her to try out these styles on you.

Stuff you might need for a hair makeover:

* Small and large butterfly clips
* Comb and brush
* Hair products (wax, gel, mousse, spray, gloss, etc.)
* Hairclips and hairgrips – all different sizes and colours
* Hairbands
* Hair jewels and beads
* Coloured hairspray and glitter

Twist and Clip

You don't need long tresses to have a hair makeover. Short hair can be funked up too.

* You will need lots of tiny butterfly clips and hair wax.
* Work the wax into your hair evenly so it has more texture.

* Next, take small sections of hair, twist back with your middle finger and hold in place with a butterfly clip.
* Spike up the ends of the hair where it is sticking up under the clip. Repeat this all over your head until you have twisted and clipped every available centimetre!

Spiketastic

This can look alarming but very cool. Your hair needs to be quite short for this to work.

* Rub lots of hair wax into your crop so it feels stiff and easy to shape. Take very small sections of hair and pinch and twist together into spikes. Repeat all over your head.
* Spray with hairspray to hold or use coloured/glitter hairspray for that added over-the-top look.

Rough With the Smooth

✱ Rub wax into your hair and then comb forward a fringe section and split into a side parting. Smooth it right down and secure the parting with a funky clip.

✱ Now you have to scrunch up the rest of the hair that isn't in the fringe parting, so that it really sticks up behind your fab smooth fringe.

✱ Spray on some hairspray to keep it in place.

For longer hair try these styles:

Tubygrip

✱ Smooth some mousse through your hair and put it into two bunches with hairbands.

✱ Leave a gap and then pull your bunch through another hairband. Leave another gap further down the bunch and repeat with a few more bands. You should be left with what resembles a plait but isn't!

✻ Leave quite a lot of hair at the ends of the bunches so you can backcomb it.

✻ This style also works well with more than just two bunches.

Snake Head

✻ Starting at the front, twist small sections of hair into a rope, clipping it with mini butterfly clips as you go along.

✻ Leave a loose tail at the end of each rope and when you have twisted all the hair at the front of your head, tie the rest, including the loose tails from the twists into a ponytail with a flowery hairband.

Curly Head

✻ Brush some mousse through damp hair. Divide the hair into lots of sections and twist each section into a little knot on top of your head.

✻ Secure each knot with a hairgrip. Don't worry if strands stick out; it will look cool.

✻ Once the whole head of hair is twisted up, spray with hairspray.

✱ This style looks excellent just like that, but when you take the knots out, you will be left with a head of beautiful curls!

Top Tip!
Comb olive oil or mayonnaise through dry hair and wrap in Clingfilm and a hot towel. Leave for an hour and then shampoo out – your hair will be soft and silky.

Blindfolded Makeover!

This will take a willing volunteer and one that doesn't mind looking like a dog's dinner at the end of it. The aim of the game is to try and put make-up on your victim while you are blindfolded. Here's how to do it:

✱ Put all the make-up into a bowl so it is easy to grab hold of.

✱ You are not allowed to use lipliners, eyeliners or mascara in case you poke them in the victim's eyes.

✱ No one is allowed to speak or give clues.

✱ The victim isn't allowed to clean the make-up off until bedtime!

CHAPTER FOUR
Action Stations

If you haven't all passed out from eating too much and laughing at each other in the makeover chair, then there is still plenty of time to play some games or even to get creative and make some cool stuff.

Cream-Cracker Relay

Make sure you have a glass of water before you play this game!

✤ Divide the sleepover party into two teams.

✤ Ask a grown-up (or one of you) to be the starter and cheat detector.

✤ At one end of the room, leave two identical piles of cream crackers. Make a 'start line' at the other end of the room.

✤ Both teams must stand behind the start line and when the starter says 'go', the first person in each team has to race to their pile of cream crackers, eat one and then run back when they have finished it.

✤ In order to prove they have finished it they

must stick out their tongue before they set off back to the rest of the team.

✤ They have to tag the next player, who has to repeat the process all over again. The team that completes the task first wins the game.

✤ If you don't have enough people for a relay, play 'race the clock' instead (this is actually worse!). Each player has to eat as many cream crackers as they can in a minute without drinking anything. It is really, really hard!

The Name Game

You will need paper torn into loads of strips to write on. All of you have to sit down and write out as many names of well-known people as you can think of: celebrities, people from history, teachers at school and so on. Screw the bits of paper into little balls and put them all in a bowl. Now you can play . . .

✤ Divide yourselves into two or three teams. One person needs to be the timekeeper and scorer. Or you can ask a brother or sister.

✤ Each player takes a name out of the bowl and has to explain who the person is to the rest of the team, without actually saying their name (or saying what the name rhymes with!).

❁ As soon as the team has guessed the name, the player takes another from the bowl. They have 2 minutes to describe as many names as they can. The names are not put back in the bowl.

❁ You can pass and choose another name only once in the 2 minutes.

❁ The winner is the team that guesses the most names without cheating!

Musical Bad-taste Clothes

Like musical chairs but much funnier!

❁ Get a bin bag and fill it with hideous clothes borrowed from parents, siblings or the dressing-up box!

❊ Everyone sits in a circle, while someone is in charge of the music.

❊ Start off by passing the bag round the circle and, when the music stops, the person with the bag has to put on an article of clothing from inside it over their own clothes!

❊ Keep playing until all the clothes are gone. The person with the most clothes loses.

Truth or Dare

This is probably the most played sleepover game in the history of sleepovers – ever! It may even be the law that you have to play it . . .

❊ Everybody has to sit round in a circle. The party hostess starts by asking 'Truth or dare?' to whoever she wants.

❊ The person answering has to choose either to answer the truth or to take on a dare, before knowing what the question is going to be.

❊ The types of questions you ask are totally up to you. You could ask if anyone has got a secret crush or have they ever wet their pants – embarrassing stuff like that makes it more cringeworthy.

✤ If the person refuses to tell the truth, they automatically have to do a dare.

✤ Dares are made up by the person asking the questions. Embarrassing ones are best. You could try getting someone to run round the house/garden with a pair of knickers on their head, or get them to wear all their clothes inside out with the most vile make-up on, then go and ask the hostess's parents for a glass of water. A good one is to dare someone to put make-up on the hostess's little brother or sister while they are asleep.

✤ The dares have to be immediate. For example, you can't ask someone to do a dare at school on Monday morning

✤ You are only allowed to appeal against a dare once. If you refuse to do it, another must be thought up and you MUST do it!

Other Games:

🌸 Board games are a good idea at sleepovers. You can get everyone to bring their favourite and you can all have a go at playing.

🌸 Twister is also a necessity at sleepovers. Everyone knows how to play it and you can make it harder for players by blindfolding them or not allowing certain body parts to be used in the game.

🌸 Hide-and-seek in the dark is always good fun and a bit spooky.

🌸 Quizzes are always a giggle. So why not buy a jumbo quiz book and divide into teams, with one of you being the quiz master?

🌸 Limbo dancing is a laugh a minute, and good if you are having a Hawaiian luau. You will need a long piece of rope or skipping rope and two of you will have to hold it tight at either end. Put on some music and hold the rope up really high so that everyone can dance under it. The aim is to keep setting the rope lower and lower until just one winner is left. You are only allowed to dance under the rope by bending backwards and if you fall over or touch the floor, you are out!

Time to Get Spooky!

All good sleepovers need to have a bit of spookiness about them or it wouldn't be a proper sleepover. Ghost stories, spooky games and sitting in torchlight are a must . . .

Murder in the Dark

A great game to play at any sleepover, especially at Halloween.

❋ Rip up as many strips of paper as there are people at the party. On one write 'Murderer', on another write 'Detective' and on the rest write 'Suspect'.

❋ Screw up all the bits of paper and put them in a bowl. Everyone must pick one and not reveal who they are, apart from the detective, who must then switch off the lights before leaving the room.

✤ Everybody then mills about in the dark room until the murderer strikes. They kill someone by putting their hand on the victim's shoulder. The victim has to scream (thus scaring everyone else to death!) and drop 'dead' on the floor.

✤ The detective comes back into the room and switches on the lights, then has to guess who the murderer is. They do this by asking everyone questions. They can ask as many questions as they like, but obviously NOT 'Are you the murderer?' That would be too easy!

✤ If you are the detective, you could ask where the suspect was standing at the time of the murder, or if they saw anything, or if anyone jumped position before the lights came on.

✤ The detective only gets one guess at the murderer, and if they guess wrongly, the murderer has won.

Mystery Objects

This game never fails to get everyone screaming!

✤ You will need to have all this organized way before everyone turns up, as you don't want anyone seeing what you have in store for them!

❋ Find as many objects as you can that have weird textures or creepy things like fake rubber spiders, snakes, bats and other things like that from the joke shop. Weird textures are easier than you think. For example: cut-up fruit like fresh figs and peeled/tinned lychees (they feel like eyeballs!) are foul when you don't know what they are. And so is cold tinned spaghetti in a bowl – it could be worms!

❋ Rub cooking oil on the fake snakes and spiders to make them feel slippery and slimy!

❋ Cooked vegetables can also feel weird when you don't know what they are. A whole cooked head of broccoli or cauliflower could be a brain . . .

❋ When you are ready to play the game, switch out all the lights and make everyone sit in a circle. One by one, each person has to guess what one of your objects is by feeling it with their hands.

❋ Start off using easy things like apples, keys or cutlery. When you have had an easy round and everyone is lulled into a false sense of security, start bringing out the bad boys!

❋ If someone doesn't guess the object, it gets passed to the person on their right. The winner is the one who has guessed the most objects.

Spooky Story Time

This is how to make up a group spooky story that will get everyone screaming with laughter.

❋ Tape together about four bits of A4 paper so they are like a long scarf. Now let your imaginations run wild!

❋ The first person to write at the top of the paper has to start the story off with the words: 'It was a dark and windy night . . .' and then continues the story from there.

❋ Each person must write a short paragraph about five lines long. When the first person has written a paragraph, they must fold over their story, leaving the last line visible for the next person to carry on where they left off. No one must be able to see the rest of the story.

🌸 Carry on like this until everyone has written their piece – the last person obviously must write an ending.

🌸 When you have finished, someone must read out the finished story by torchlight in the dark room.

If anyone knows any good ghost stories, make them tell those as well, with all the lights switched off and their face uplighted by a torch. Scary stuff!

On a Lighter Note . . . Sleepover Idol!

We all know those cheesy TV talent shows that discover the next big star. Well, how about hosting your own talent night right there in your living room?

All you need is a karaoke CD and a hairbrush as a microphone. The words to the songs should be printed on the inside of the CD cover. Everyone chooses their song and takes turns to sing while the others sit back and enjoy the show.

To make it more interesting, you could write scores out of ten on pieces of A4 paper and hold them up at the end of each person's party piece. The winner has to do an encore of a different song.

Why not have a dance-off as well? Each of you has 5 minutes to think of a dance routine to a piece of music, and has to perform it in front of everyone. Let's hope those break-dance moves are up to scratch . . .

Movie Magic

No sleepover would be complete without watching at least one movie on DVD. But how can you be sure you will rent one that all your guests like?

Easy! When you send out the invite for the party, attach an RSVP with the choice of five movies and ask each girl to tick the one she likes best. The two films with the most votes are hired and that way you should just about please everyone.

What do you think the top five sleepover movies are?

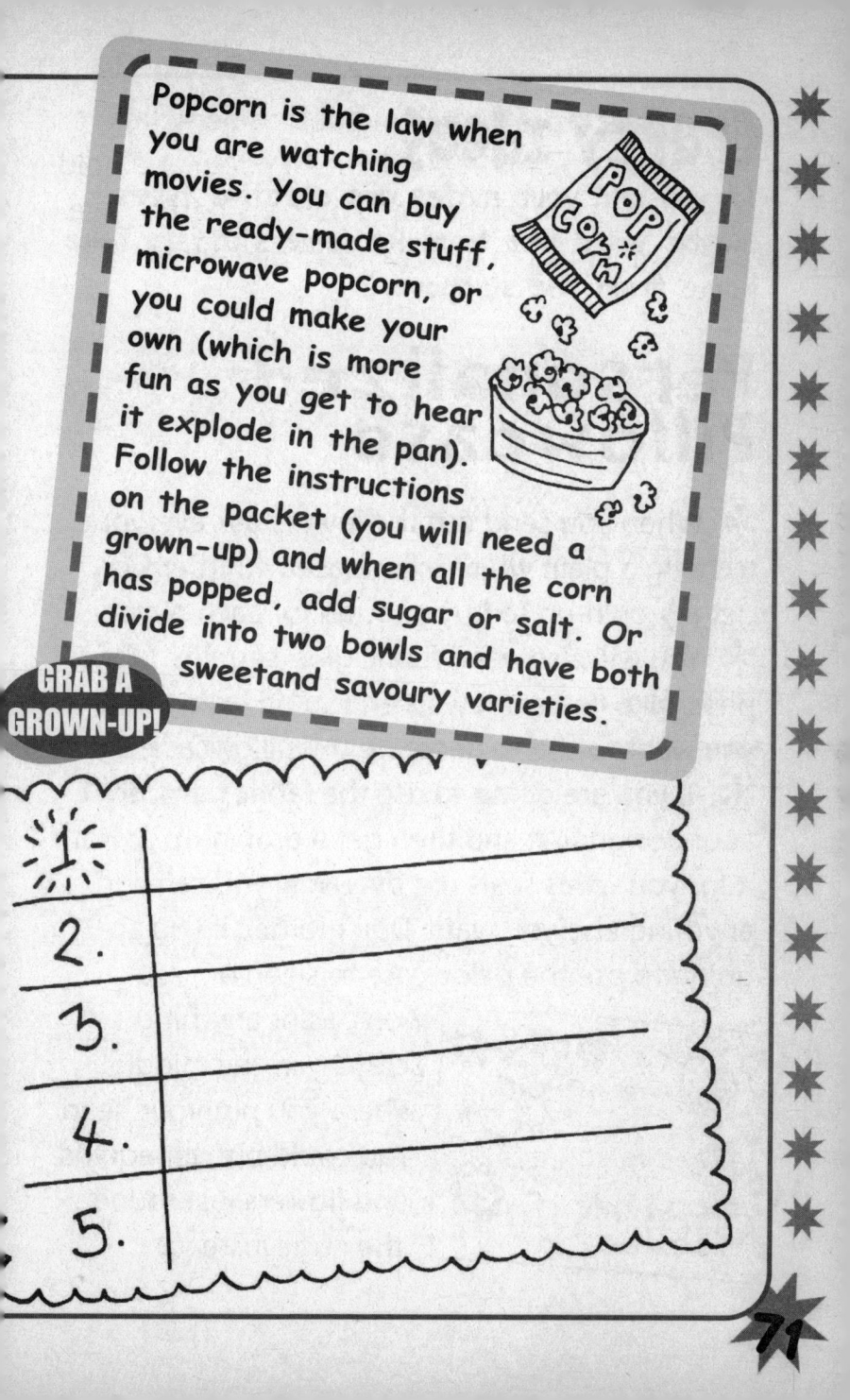

Popcorn is the law when you are watching movies. You can buy the ready-made stuff, microwave popcorn, or you could make your own (which is more fun as you get to hear it explode in the pan). Follow the instructions on the packet (you will need a grown-up) and when all the corn has popped, add sugar or salt. Or divide into two bowls and have both sweet and savoury varieties.

GRAB A GROWN-UP!

1.
2.
3.
4.
5.

Crafty Ideas

If you and your mates are creative types, maybe you'd like to make some stuff to take home from the sleepover?

Personalized Pillowcase

- When you send out the invites, ask everyone to bring a plain white pillowcase with them, or get a grown-up to buy enough for each of you.
- You will also need fabric glue, sequins, fabric pens, fake flowers, jewels and so on – anything you want to use to decorate the pillowcase.
- If you are going to use the fabric pens, do your design first and then get a grown-up to iron it for you – this seals the dye. Now you can add anything else you want. Don't forget, if you are going to use the pillowcase to sleep on, you won't want anything scratchy in the middle where you put your head. You could put all sequins and flowers just round the edge instead.

Old TS: New Life

It's not just our faces that need makeovers – our clothes can get tired and boring too! If you have an old T-shirt kicking about at home that you just don't wear any more because it has lost its appeal, why not give it a facelift?

- At haberdashery or department stores you can buy the most amazing beading, sequins, feather trims, fringes, fabric badges or flowers. You name it, it will be there, and it's all fairly cheap.
- See if everyone can bring along something like that and then you will have a huge selection of glittery stuff to choose from.
- Fabric glue is a wonderful thing and will stick down leather and any other material as if it has been stitched with wrought iron. Be careful not to stick your fingers together, though!

✣ Trim the bottom of old Ts with sequins, feather trim, fringe or beaded string. Decorate the neckline and round the armholes.

✣ Buy glittery fabric pens and make up whole designs, repeating patterns all over the T.

✣ You can buy iron-on military badges and transfers – get a grown-up to help out here.

GRAB A GROWN-UP!

✣ Cut the arms off the T to make a vest and cut across the neckline to make it a slash-neck top.

✣ Cut off one of the arms diagonally across the neckline and cut the other arm off at the stitching to make an asymmetrical top. Glue a bow made from gorgeous ribbon on to the shoulder that is still there.

✣ You could do a makeover swap and get someone else to makeover your T-shirt for you while you do someone else's too.

Tired jeans

Have you got a pair of jeans that hide at the back of the wardrobe in a sad heap because you don't love them any more? Try these quick fixes . . .

- Cut the waistband off the jeans and make them low slung.
- Cut about 5 centimetres off the bottom, fold the ends over a few times, then get a grown-up to iron down the turn-up. Now you have trendy three-quarter turn-ups that go well with flip-flops!

GRAB A GROWN-UP!

- For party jeans, glue sequins and beads on the pockets. You could also glue sequin trim down the sides on the seam.
- Cut the seam open on the outside of each leg as far as your knee. Don't worry if they are a bit crooked – when you wash them they will fray and look really cool. You will need a willing grown-up for the next part. Snip small holes about 3–4 centimetres apart in the fabric all the way up either side of the seam you have just cut open – these are your lace holes. You will need a really long piece of ribbon/leather

string/sequinned string or something similar to use as a shoelace. Thread through the holes and – *voilà* – you have instant lace-up jeans!

❋ With glitter fabric pens, draw any design you want, such as a flower, star or butterfly, starting at the bottom of each leg and fading out around about the knees of the jeans. Dot on jewels and sequins to add extra sparkle.

More Quick Crafty Ideas

❋ Take an old belt you never wear and glue on sequins, jewels and beads to give it an instant makeover.

❋ Plait together very long pieces of different coloured ribbon and tie at the ends, leaving quite a big tail of loose ribbon to dangle down when you tie it round your waist as a cool new belt. You can do the same for a ribbon choker and friendship bracelets but just make the pieces of ribbon much shorter.

❋ Plain bargain basement flip-flops can be funked up by gluing on jewels and fake flowers at half the price of the ones in the trendy shops. You could all make a pair for each other!

✣ Decorate plain wooden photo frames with beads and shells or sweets (like the sweetie invite in Chapter One) and seal with a layer of clear varnish. Frame a picture from the sleepover to remember a great night.

✣ Cover old shoeboxes with millions of beads and sequins and some fluffy trim to make keepsake boxes for storing those all-important bits of jewellery and secret notes.

Time capsule

Wouldn't it be amazing if you could look back in time and see what you had been doing at a particular moment, what you had been thinking and what your secret wishes had been? That's what a time capsule is for!

Why not make one as a keepsake of your night together and ask a grown-up to keep it in a safe place for when you are ready to take a peek and check out those embarrassing tastes in boy bands and hideous clothes.

❋ First, you will need a box to put the keepsakes in – so why not make one from a shoebox as described earlier?

❋ You could include a sample of anything you made on the night, like a necklace or bracelet – though not food, obviously! Or a list of the movies you watched and the games you played. The invite has to go in as well!

❋ Make a menu of the food you scoffed and keep that too.

❋ If one of you has brought an instant camera, you could take lots of photos and put a few of those inside.

❋ A very cool thing to do is for each of you to fill in a questionnaire about your likes and dislikes, who your fave bands are – that sort of thing. If you have access to a computer, you could type one out and make copies for everyone to complete.

❋ Your sleepover time capsule questionnaire could look something like this:

Name:

....
....

Age:

....

Date and time:

....

Draw a self-portrait:

Your favourite animal:

....

Your favourite band/pop star:

....

Your favourite food:

....

If you had three wishes, what would they be?

....
....
....

If you could be anything in the world, what would you be?

....

Who is your best friend?

....

Dogs or cats?

....

Boys – a pain or OK?

....

Do you have a crush on anyone?

....

Trainers or shoes?

....

Jeans or trackies?

....

Glitter – good or baaaaad?

....

Name of your fave teddy?

....

What are you wearing right now?

....

What was the last thing you ate?

....

Basically – you just ask as many nosy questions as you want and see if they get answered!

CHAPTER FIVE
The Morning After

Wake up, sleepyheads, the party isn't over, you know! You did go to bed last night, didn't you? Hmm ... But now it's morning and you all need to eat lots to give you energy to tidy up! The fun doesn't stop just yet ...

Breakfast Fit for Princesses

Apparently, this is the most important meal of the day, so why not make your sleepover breakfast into a real occasion? Push the boat out and have more than just cereal and toast. Croissants, muffins, bagels, *pain au chocolat* and brioche are all yummy sleepover favourites, but why not make some other stuff as well?

Fried Cinnamon Toast

You will need:
Sliced white or brown bread
125g softened butter
125g brown sugar
2 teaspoons ground cinnamon

GRAB A GROWN-UP!

☕ Make sure the butter is really soft for this or it could be a bit tricky. You may need more butter and sugar if you have lots of people.

☕ Cream together the butter, sugar and cinnamon in a bowl with a wooden spoon, or you could cheat and ask a grown-up to chuck it all in the blender.

☕ Spread the mixture on both sides of the bread and then heat up a frying pan.

☕ Fry the bread on both sides until lightly toasted and serve with more cinnamon butter or with slices of banana.

Eggy Bread

GRAB A GROWN-UP!

You will need:
Sliced white bread
6 eggs
Dash of milk
Knob of butter

☕ Whisk the eggs together in a bowl and pour in a splash of milk to thin slightly.

☕ Heat the butter in a frying pan and dip the sliced bread into the bowl with the eggs, making sure it is completely covered on both sides.

☕ Fry the bread in the pan on both sides until golden and keep warm until you have used up all the egg mixture.

☕ You can season with salt, pepper and ketchup, sprinkle on sugar, drizzle on honey or maple syrup or top with crispy bacon. Anything is possible with eggy bread!

Pancakes

These are fun to make – try flipping them and see who drops the most!

You will need:
- 100 g plain flour
- 2 eggs
- 150 ml milk
- 150 ml water
- 1–2 tablespoons of melted butter or sunflower oil
- oil or melted butter for frying

GRAB A GROWN-UP!

☕ Either blend all the ingredients together in a food processor or place the flour in a bowl, mix in the eggs and gradually beat in the milk, water and melted butter until you have a smooth batter.

☕ Brush a frying pan with butter or oil and heat over a high heat. You will know it is hot enough if you splash a drop of water in there and it sizzles away.

☕ Remove the pan from the heat and pour in 2 tablespoons of batter for a thin pancake and more for a thicker one. Tip the pan as you pour, so you completely coat the base.

☕ Return the pan to the heat and cook for about 30 seconds, then turn the pancake over using a fish slice or palette knife. Or you could be brave and get a grown-up to show you how to flip it – but be prepared for mess and failure if you do! Cook until golden that side too.

☕ Stack the pancakes up in a warm oven until you have finished and then get busy with fillings: chocolate spread, jam, lemon juice and sugar, grated cheese and sliced tomato, chopped-up banana and raisins, honey, maple syrup, golden syrup . . .

☕ Spread on your filling and then roll into a tube and eat hot.

☕ If you want chocolate pancakes, replace 2 teaspoons of the flour with 2 teaspoons of cocoa powder.

The Best Hot Chocolate in the World... EVER

Breakfast won't be complete without this . . .

You will need:
Enough milk for all of you
cocoa powder (unsweetened)
Sugar
1 large bag marshmallows

GRAB A GROWN-UP!

☕ Measure out the milk into a mug and pour into a big pan – repeat for however many people there are.

☕ While the milk is heating on the cooker, heat up the grill and place all the marshmallows on a baking tray and toast them both sides.

☕ When the milk has started bubbling slightly, take the pan off the heat and add the cocoa powder. The rule is generally 2 teaspoons of cocoa per person. Get someone to count for you or you will mess it up after no sleep!

☕ Whisk with a hand whisk or fork until the chocolate is mixed in and then pour into mugs. People can add their own sugar – 2–3 teaspoons will be plenty.

☕ When the sugar has been stirred in, dunk the toasted marshmallows on top and drink up. Yum!

Party Favours

Traditionally, a sleepover ends with everyone walking away with a little something to remember the night by. You don't have to do this, of course, but it is a nice touch and sure to make your sleepover stand out a mile from everyone else's!

You could make your party favours or you could just buy little gifts and hand them out in party bags or cheap gift boxes.

Ideas:

Friendship bracelets (plaiting together three different coloured ribbons)

Edible sweetie bracelets (threading Jelly Babies, Midget Gems, etc., on to a piece of elastic)

Mini picture frame or mirror jazzed up with beads and glitter, etc.

A cool key ring

Gorgeous lipgloss

Facial glitter and nail tattoos

Nail varnish

Earrings

Hair accessories

Mini teddy

Bye-bye and Thank You

The most important thing to remember about a sleepover is to clear up after yourselves, because you want the grown-ups to let you have another one, don't you? It is a good idea to send your parents or guardian a little thank-you note as well. Grown-ups love all that! And if you have been to a sleepover, please don't forget to send a thank-you note to the hostess or you may not be invited again! You can make your own (always much appreciated!) or buy one. It doesn't matter, as long as you do it.

Have a fab night! You see, there's no need to get stressed out. Having a sleepover is the most fun ever. Here's to becoming the sleepover queen and holding the best parties in town!

Template for page 16

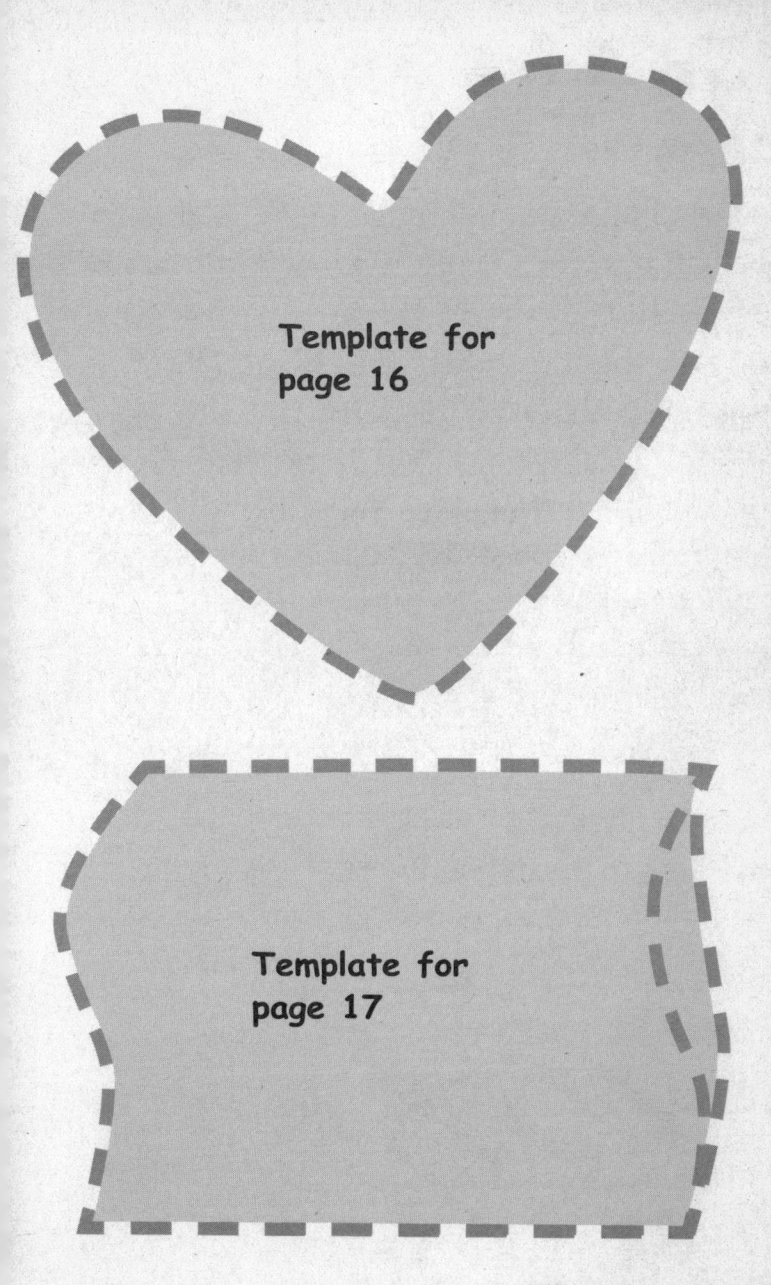

Template for page 17

Template for
page 18